"Continuing the lofty tradition of Langston Hughes, June Jordan, and Amiri Baraka, Tongo Eisen-Martin has emerged on center stage as today's premier revolutionary poet. A master craftsman and a sensitive artist, he reserves his sledgehammer words for the cruelty of imperialism. He should not only be read — he should be studied."
— Gerald Horne

"'Revolution' appears at least two dozen times in Tongo Eisen-Martin's amazing *Blood on the Fog*. Find something like a revolving, reiterating locomotion of music riding the rails of thinking and feeling in *Blood on the Fog*. Find a poetry of 'swinging type body language' where the swinging swings like Ellington and Ali combined, knocking you out inside and out, and turning you around in this extraordinary book."
— Terrance Hayes

"One of the inimitable operations here is to recalibrate the relationship with, Tongo writes, 'streets,' or 'corner' or 'city.' It's a fact, therefore, that the poems stage a wild meta-conversation regarding the presumption that Black people are external to the art being practiced, the art in question. The flat terms of our dying are plainly in need of morphogenesis. Police. Bullet. Prison. I mean: 'Baby, if God doesn't care about what you are writing, it is time to un-die.' Black poetry has got to get its head around the deranged way language and the world expect us to be and live again. Tongo has figured this out, is feeling out how one might poem with his own life, and that's v
— Simone White

BLOOD ON THE FOG

BLOOD ON THE FOG

Tongo Eisen-Martin

Pocket Poets Series : Number 62
City Lights Books | San Francisco

Cover art: Biko Eisen-Martin

Some of the poems in this collection were printed in the following: *Santa Clara Review*, *Lana Turner Journal*, *e-flux journal*, Poetry Foundation, *Dryland*, *Jewish Currents*, *The Rumpus*, *Harper's Magazine*, poets.org, and *Commune Magazine*.

Library of Congress Cataloging-in-Publication Data

Names: Eisen-Martin, Tongo, author.
Title: Blood on the fog / by Tongo Eisen-Martin.
Description: San Francisco : City Lights Books, 2021. | Series: Pocket poets series
Identifiers: LCCN 2021011704 | ISBN 9780872868755 (paperback)
Subjects: LCGFT: Poetry.
Classification: LCC PS3605.I8275 B58 2021 | DDC 811/.6--dc23
LC record available at https://lccn.loc.gov/2021011704

ISBN: 978-0-87286-875-5

City Lights Books are published at the City Lights Bookstore
261 Columbus Avenue, San Francisco, CA 94133.
www.citylights.com

CONTENTS

For my mother

A Good Earth

I talk facing away from the dead
They replace me with the change in my pocket
A penny that has yet to be invented

They say, "You have to know how to cut a throat on the way to
    cutting a throat"

After sleeping on a mattress made from two garbage bags of clothes
I became content with the small gestures of plantation fires

Playing with couch ashes, I realized how weird the universe was. It
exists in so many places. So many random things. It interrupts me
when I am trying to dream. Like your clay correspondence, Lord

To be transparent
I have twenty books next to a bullet
Like an old man giving advice at the beginning of a revolution

I've really done it, Lord. Explored the mumbles of my mind.
Explored what's naturally there. And I found no brainwashing. I
found Africa, Lord

I have a future
It takes place in the diasporic South
I have morning possessions
Modern militancy
I mean windows to the South
I will walk on a missile for food

I guess you will not want flowers for a few years, Lord

Will I be tied face to face with the country I murder

Merge with us, Lord

Our old metal vs. the new metal
Our old metal vs. a pool of meandering imperialist faces
A multiculturalism of sorts

The dead replace me with a comedian's chest cavity
Instead of a chest cavity held tight

It takes a violent middleman for me to talk to myself
Stories that travel through other people's stories
A song about a song
A hemisphere about a hemisphere
Stories that travel through a conquered poet

My mother remembers Africa, Lord
She killed on behalf of you, Lord

I wore a machete all winter and no one asked me what it meant
I read one thousand books in front of the world

What I do is fight poems

And sleep through decadent San Francisco prayer circles

Watch people play for post-working-class associative surfaces

Or re-creations of a governor's desk
Ruling-class art of utility
Playing find the sociopathic bureaucrat

A day white people scare even easier
TV in a basket next to a ceramic baby
Wearing ceramic armor
Musket progeny fantasizing through the art of the poor
Their trendy latches locked before God
Black art hunted down like a dog

Hand over my friends, Lord

Lord, I think that I am going to die in a war

Unelected white people in my small house
Like a blues song of no spiritual affect
Or dollhouse H-bomb
A pony show near dead bodies
Apartheid weddings that go right
Apartheid white people who give birth to mathematicians
The spiritual continuity of barracks and police stations
The chemical interpretation of a Sunday trip to church
Church smells in their pockets
A river mistaken for a talking river
No autobiography outside of small personal victories of violence
    and drug use
Made in the image of God's trinkets
What white abolitionists confided in their children about
Chemical assurances that

They will switch from Black artist to white artist
Black God to white God
Black worker to white worker

I think about you cautiously, Lord
In the same way I think about my childhood, Lord

Foxhole Friday nights
Most of life is mute

Comedian points out a planter's field to the priest

King sugar cane
King cotton
King revolutionary

The bottle is central
Containing all modes of shallow introduction
Introducing an unlisted planter class
Speaking about fever and balance sheets
And reassuring the masses
That we can figure out our fathers later

A priest took my mother lightly, Lord
Stood in front of the parishioners re-raveling
Fantasies about Black art
Priest reading confidently
Before I broke him
And broke his parallel

After today, I have never been a poet before

A little brother watches his big brother's friends
They lean rifles on shelter walls
They agree with me and call it literature

It's a simple matter this revolution thing
To really lie to no one
To keep nothing godlike

To write a poem for God

I Do Not Know the Spelling of Money

I go to the railroad tracks
And follow them to the station of my enemies

A cobalt-toothed man pitches pennies at my mugshot negative

All over the united states, there are
                              toddlers in the rock

I see why everyone out here got in the big cosmic basket
And why blood agreements mean a lot
And why I get shot back at

I understand the psycho-spiritual refusal to write white history
    or take the glass freeway

                    White skin tattooed on my right forearm
                    Ricochet sewage near where I collapsed
                            into a rat-infested manhood

My new existence as living graffiti

                            In the kitchen with
                    a lot of gun cylinders to hack up
                            House of God in part
                                No cops in part

                    My body brings down the Christmas

The new bullets pray over blankets made from old bullets

Pray over the 28th hour's next beauty mark

Extrajudicial confederate statue restoration
The waistband before the next protest poster

                              By the way,
              Time is not an illusion, your honor
                I will save your desk for last
                  You are witty, your honor
           You're moving money again, your honor

It is only raining one thing: non-white cops

        And prison guard shadows
              Reminding me of
              Spoiled milk floating on an oil spill

        A neighborhood making a lot of fuss over its demise

        A new lake for a Black Panther Party

Malcom X's ballroom jacket slung over my son's shoulders
                The figment of village
              A noon noose to a new white preacher
                  — all in an abstract painting of a president

Bought slavers some time, didn't it?
The tantric screeches of military bolts and Election-Tuesday cars

A cold-blooded study in leg irons

Proof that some white people have actually fondled nooses
        That sundown couples
            made their vows of love over
                    opaque peach plastic
                    and bolt-action audiences

The Medgar Evers Second is definitely my favorite law of science

Fondled news clippings and primitive Methodists

My arm changes imperialisms
Simple policing vs. Structural frenzies
Elementary school script vs. Even whiter white spectrums

Artless bleeding and
the challenge of watching civilians think

                "Terrible rituals they have around the corner.
                    They let their elders beg for public mercy"

    "I am going to go ahead and sharpen these kids' heads into
        arrows myself and see how much gravy spills out of family
        crests."

Modern fans of war
        What with their T-shirt poems
        And T-shirt guilt

And me, with the cheapest pair of shoes on the bus,
I have no choice but to read the city walls for signs of my life

The Possibility of Being One Person

*I had this dream (planted dead in a weekday) that I was laid up in
the hospital. And people kept coming into my room by the dozens.
And each dozen had special handshakes for each other
and occasionally current dance moves.*

*And they would kick my hospital bed from time to time to let me
know that they would be dancing from this hospital room on out to
my grave. Strange cha cha's and soft shoe shuffles. Disco spins. Like
they were dancing for a white sundial marking numbness in their
feet-drum-race-riot.*

*And I was ready to die, because you know, ask a musician
in the tombs after court:
It's the surroundings that is the uniform.*

. . . But I just couldn't bring myself to visualize against God.

*One of them stood over me like a conductor waving their arms over
my body, directing my heart to beat fainter and fainter. Directing the
tubes to turn the fluids back. And I faded from consciousness with
thud after thud on the legs of my bed as they
danced wilder and wilder.*

*Well, wild but meek. Or artificially meek. Like an artificial pastor
told them to be. I was to be a projection or some kind of character
to be laid at their feet. "You are the only one participating in the
revolution today," they mocked. And I was ready to go because, you
know, there are plenty of pianos that could use a new soul. And I'm*

thinking we were supposed to be in the revolution as long as it takes.
So you can punch me out now. I was born with one foot
in a lime pit anyway.

But, check it out, no one bothered to ask the doctor if I was really
dead. Too busy strutting. Too busy kissing. And I kept fading and
fading. With only enough breath and sweet consciousness to count
their smiles. One. Two. Three. Four. Five. And then I heard a voice.
A whisper. And it was counting with me. Six, we said. Seven, we said.

Eight . . . and then another joined us. Nine. Ten. Then another.

I haven't been eating, momma.
I've been in a trance.
I haven't been sleeping.
I've been washing my hands off of the Port of Charleston.

There is blood on the fog.

Sunday

Monk put the universe back into its mind
                              remembering God alone

I'm crying in the corner of a Pittsburgh room
Spelling numbers to myself
                              when she calls

Plain love
I see one hundred of her in the room
And the playwright gone

I'm making a dash for a country-less train
She reaches me before the air / Barely above water
                              but I would rather
                              keep track of the sky

"No, the sun is the other way. And I could have sworn that
the floor was pointing at itself in agreement. And I was full of
indescribable love and real spirits even let me choose between tears
and laughter."

Skeleton crew doing two hundred years of work in the playhouse
and I quit the brightest notes to come sit by you

She loves me while my soul doubles then halves then
doubles in muscle memory
                              — a delta, it's the kindness

A Sketch about Genocide

A San Francisco police chief says, "Yes, you poets make points.
    But they are all silly."

Police chief sewing a mouth onto a mouth
Police chief looking straight through the poet

Flesh market both sides of the levee
Change of plans both sides of the nonviolence

                    On no earth
                    Just an earth character

His subordinate says, "Awkward basketball moves look good on
you, sir . . . Yes, we are everywhere, sir . . . yes, unfortunately for
now, white people only have Black History . . . we will slide the
wallpaper right into their cereal bowls, sir . . . Surveil the shuffle."

I am a beggar and all of this day is too easy
I want to see all of the phases of a wall
Every age it goes through
                    Its humanity
                    Its environmental racism

We call this the ordeal blues
Now crawl to the piano seat and make a blanket for your cell
Paint scenes of a child dancing up to the court appearance
And leaving a man,
                    but not for home

Atlantic Ocean charts mixed in with parole papers
Mainstream funding (the ruling class's only pacifism)

Ruling class printing judges (fiat kangaroos)
Making judges hand over fist
Rapture cop packs and opposition whites all above a thorny stem
Caste plans picked out like vans for the murder show
Anglo-saints addicting you to a power structure

You want me to raise a little slave, don't you?
Bash his little brain in
And send him to your civil rights

No pain
Just a white pain

Delicate bullets in a box next to a stack of monolith scriptures
(makes these bullets look relevant, don't it?)

I remember you
Everywhere you lay your hat is the capital of the south
The posture you introduced to that fence
The fence you introduced to political theory

If you shred my dreams, son
I will tack you to gun smoke

The suburbs are finally offended

This will be a meditation too

In These Swamps, a Common Name

I lied, Lord, and said I was a writer
dancing with my debts in front of my children
a semi-circle of cargo-flesh — your good and righteous oasis, Lord

Lord, they want to pick fights
        with a loner
Trigger-men jubilation
           (albeit a clumsy one)
                Muttering bargain-basement thralls at my car

The nickel smell of waking up in terror every raggedy fall

"I am building a revolution right next to you, trigger-man . . .
   What slave do you identify with?"

The sweetest, sweetest key: for a fraction of a second, you were the
   most violent person on earth

Becoming a leader was fairly seamless
All you have to do is open yourself to all of your fear — those
   errands for the drinking gourd

Don't repeat your neighborhood to anyone

That's my cousin eulogized now in literary history . . . wasn't pretty . . .
    this effect on my eternal soul

I tried to cry on the side (face in a sink full of alcohol)

Fine flowers of struggle
            color spectrum the cousin
                        who is dead if you brace yourself

It's hard to write without my friend

No Malcolm positions on East Coast warfare
            My friend — in the audience with the earth's coming mood

Mainland jazz

The organizing is all over me
Let me divine you the Lenox Ave. of the future . . . the river just keeps
    riding freights town to town

Violent revolution in this very year

            Open your paper to us

Rulers of the night train
Your humble dishwashers who lived to hum the details

To look into the future like a gentleperson

Three-fifths of a typewriter

Do some math with me here in the absence of confidence
        The luxuries of a paranoia that you can finish later

                        My friend died yesterday

Like belated parenting, we haunt each other in quick bursts now

Sample the drug
Wrestle the angel
No depth of setting

Hiding behind the hordes because I'm in the train business
You don't need a ticket for a winter that only happened here

    (Behind this room is my mind/ashes runneth over
    Throwing around this room is my mind/brim of an innocent soul)

Which dollar deserves my neck?

Thinking about you is like sharing a ghost with half of the city's afterlife
Thinking about you centers us

I'm just a small man in a basement window chronicling material
    conditions
Boiling water next to a change in the course of poor people's consciousness

I cannot impress you with the names of guns
Another city ends

We haunt each other with absolute pragmatism
With the truth of Afrikan transcendence

We hear the fire out
"I never really did like the car they found me in"
              Imagine what defines a creature

Where remnants of concrete put none of the world down
Except slabs of a deadbeat nationalism
Or a bloodline making the news again

True, I have an absence of style

        Just a doorstep moving dead body to dead body

The Sideman on the Canvas

My failing as a jail spirit

Or specific custody for me, Monk
Almost a fist through the marquee
They beat me like old pearls into riverbanks of an assortment of
    Black latitudes

So many stabbed-up instruments

Nothing left of us, but sweet Chicago rage

1919, Monk

My first poem as a white man
And all I see is a depopulated and obedient abyss twisting to the
metronome ticks of my mother and father and baby prison society
. . . God doesn't even seem possible . . . I run every street . . . I
light every cigarette . . . I conjure body language (don't call it the
south) . . . I live in someone's terrified arms . . . there are these
1820s church pews . . . un-painting themselves . . . there are these
cracker doves . . . and the prison just keeps getting older and older
. . . and I know you have to be a genius . . . you know, invite the
devil into Reconstruction . . . you have to chase music even while
you are dying . . . my conscience is clean, but still not the blues
. . . more gallant rats . . . and the death mask that fits millions . . .

Do you find me morbid, Monk?

I woke up on a battlefield and also looking down from the crystal
    of a windchime. I was a rooftop without a city
Trying to figure out the right thing to do with my spare change
    subtext —
Clinking coins dialoguing like God's efforts

The carpenter's body was Black, right?
Underground body

Simile nothing
Abstraction nothing
[It's] society time

detested and forgiven in this universe
letting me try my mind again

The police pantry was well stocked
And there I was, not participating in street life
My hands far from the self-talk

You could actually see police leverage bobbing up and down in a
    nuclear harbor
You could see flattened massacres of Black people

The biographies done. Neatly stacked on top of my infant body
Sleeping through my first imperialist summer
    hospital floors swept up of all ten million bullets
    my conscience in drum patterns and drum patterns
    strangely perceived

no home away from police insecurities
no working-class artifacts

Just the state mythos and its love balladeers
Europe serving two masters. Maybe two hundred thousand and
    a minor Christ
    someone begging for change next to biographies
    stomachs pumped next to biographies

I had all these 7-day candles lit, Monk
and I knew I was just not getting it
the pain was just not sliding down the notes right
not saving someone's world

just odd walls of fear
asking, "what is there, actually a true self?"

between these mildly confident walls
recalling how the front of the body feels outside
social contracts well dressed
and courted shrewdly
stabbed at shrewdly

The hour begins again

I play the piano because at this point
        it doesn't matter who I have ever been before I sat
          down to play

Her fingertips wandering around the centimeters of history
    playwriting to correct my posture in this club

Met her while I was trying to make sense of a hurried paranoia
All apartments seemed to soften

No quote is out of the question on this piano

similar to a deity walking down from a mountain
I was a child on drugs
anything blue can become a train
or wander into her cigarette
I am not a storyteller / she will never be a ghost

                "You can take me back now, baby,
                now this decade is going normal"

I play the piano against itself now
I would ruin my body in this love

She smiles at her drink

      Chaos in my superstition

A Play in Two Parts

English is a lukewarm relationship with your people
>   With practice, I met every white person in the world

The state's pastel gibberish and
>   White-noise watchlists transmuted by agents who
>   point finger pistols
>   at Black children
>   . . . for funded nature

>   And now it's winter . . . or adulthood in america

Retail awards and standard-issue bullets left on a plate outside
    my door
Plate design inspired by the gold-trim razor wire around
    mother Afrika
>   — A congressional motif

Rope tickles neck

I am a human sacrifice / my parallel employment — pocket full of
    fists — defining efforts to be part of a famous family / the
    hospital bed shakes

Now I am a white man's son

To quote the people who left me for dead . . . nervous energy all
    over the constitution . . . I owe you a war

I had a firm grasp on my mortality
I had an idea for a sonnet and a prison wall all picked out

Besides the nightstick, I know no other colors today

My double grows in Mississippi
My shoulders turned towards where lesser gods landed
Where the light changes revolutions

Pure america now confronts the woman I love

Psalm sketched
A sketch of gallows foreplay
        [You've taken me back
                Your humble narrator]

Gallows bandstand
and every place she turned my life into decent artwork

Imagine us
        the death of commerce
        velvet gloves passing around our FBI file

Police station muscling for robber baron free associations
The sum of all corporate defense mechanisms

                        Maybe a pale horse hoof

Policing that don't involve populations
Just population-symbols

Rope tickles a trumpet of God's
In the beginning was the word for a little bit

Rope tickles the water

Out-evolved by the police state, the suburbs retract
Bullwhips dealt liberally in a prison society
Vice president's initials on every nightstick
          saying, "The next person out the door better mean america
          no harm"

I've been blinded by this sun sitting on the wall

Our door hinges in the water

                              I wish my imagination was formal

                    Deathtrap narrator book-burning the hospital lobby

                                        Gallows king

                              I am a revolutionary there too

Walking Around the World with this Fire

The poetry of the future is written by mothers
who know your memoir by heart

A revolutionary's laughter that becomes side door of the universe . . .
explains our take on liberation — in part — the invention of a new
motherhood
and a new universe to host it

with giant steps she learned how to use knives in america

Red Summer state of spirits
Also, pigeon imperialism expressed through a rose period

— Pick up the gun and learn something about your mind —

What else is there to do besides stop singing?

Finish letters to Vietnam then sit still

Cue empire and a monolith of mothers carrying babies
from one side of the holding cell to the other

a mountain moved into the mass soul

Don't look for a nuanced communist manifesto

walking around the world with this fire

My mother doesn't care
about your white house refund . . .
your utopia meetings

It's the devil who has been
ducking her for decades

devil hiding
with puppet-presidents
turning wine into humans

And there she was . . . keeping pace with electricity

A crowded room singing the perfect blues

Fidel near a kind word

Nuclear ego on the chopping block

Friends in need of a martial art

An atmosphere of close calls

or the whites of soldier eyes made more communal
pigs attempting to skip history
meeting their makers wearing
shades of an acceptable minor key
in industrial wine (a return)

Clenched jaw gains a reckoning

the point of creation
to keep talking about the people

Because the military industrial complex
has the lower 9th on a string
we look for you there
on all paths revolutionary

We have spirits who talk to and through you

federally surveilled early dinner and the foothills of
ancestor-possession

sleeping outside your body

mulling over revolutions

Good books floating around the room
We're talking about non-religious,
but ridiculously spiritual people
ready to tutor an imperialist's blood
ready to improve our applause

I can run to any rock

I have a mother
where there was
and will be fire

I Imitate You

Picture, 1960s newspaper clippings and teeth hanging on a string
   — *Like a book of life*

I'm in the kitchen with my would-be killer
Picking their canines out of a mouth harp
Cigarette-ing a pen
Calling Black Fire to prayer

Unscrewing the blues
I am played down

      The aim to only die for money once

Mouth harp prepared:
      Ladies and gentlemen: We know what you all are not doing.
      Mainly you all are not leaving the universe to its childhood.

A church signals another church with mirrors and nose-drips
The spirit-world up and starts murdering city trees

Our psychic re-break
sleeping-in-my-car Sunday chores
allegory of new hard R's
or folk tale about a wolf's tongue in the cartons of cheap milk

Trace amounts of white sheet on a politician's teleprompter
A glass case grows in Brooklyn
Lower Ninth Ward houses play hopscotch and leapfrog like
    white children

While cops wave their bills at the world

The news cameras follow
          a teenager's descent into hell

I have grown up a little bit lately
Almost becoming inanimate will do that for you

Activist peril and new-millennium jug music
or the bottle you'd rather throw at your head than drink

No going to regular-people jail / no being hunted by regular-
      people cops
"Believe In the Street" is my first thought
                          Is my parallel first name

A feat in spiritual equilibrium, I am waiting for God in front of a
      container factory

Put another way:
Yawning after a night in jail feels like keeping busy
feels like imitating yourself severely
a bar code no more
nor new junkie's angst
one step ahead of every plantation owner in your pocket

The Lord's blues
I am eating every imagination in the room
Looking through Camden windows with perfect Zen concentration
I understand the constitution and all the drugs it promised

Looking at shapes martyred by an imperialist state
Jail barges on a grandmother's table
Couple poems away from your class suicide

"May the white citizens council steady your hand."
        artists ordered to embroider "Enemy of the people" onto
           millions of pillowcases.

Aiyana Jones sewn into body temperatures
A cue to cook Brooklyn
          Children watching and identifying with people
             The man you made out of a face card
             The most uncooperative object in a cell

Police state only a few inches from your address
             I talked to a class-less people today
      They were not essentially overworked nor military captains
      They were not wage-washed nor inbred in a Victorian series

          Maybe I am the last white man on earth

             All I dream is physical death
          Thinking about God / and God empty

In clumps of prison, my poem
        my cubist-remade scar
        my Saturn for adults
        my junkie industrialism

I knew my father as much as I want to be known

Free Fear

The boss belongs to the masses now
Got the boss's likeness on a string like a love poem
Wild stride speeches replace memories of the boss
We got machine guns in the communist bar tonight
We are naturals in the communist bar
Our boundaries are just a little death

We stand outside the gates of San Francisco
                listening to some good preaching

            "Congratulations, your mercenaries hurt.
        Your Money Jungle hurts. Your mouths hurt."

              "Merchants of frenetic white flight
     Luckless and (therefore) well-armed primitivism
       reaching down into the patterns of your soul
                 making for funny stories"

            "I hope they didn't name any schools
         while they had those kids in those cages"

Joy returns to decent revolutionaries
          Puts a hermitage in the fascism

Saint Fallujah thumping, your shoulder is family
                 and needed
God crawling in between the bullet heat
Yes, our grandparents' God
Thought experiments in the last words of Black organizers

Let's make a periodical of their last words, Lord
of the remaining addresses of Black power

We become Angola on both sides / A humor of axes
A foot race through public property / remilitarized
Pork improved / celestial pork
Platinum-minted pork / choose your words carefully pork

"the first mirror was clay . . . the first human was not"

Humanity recommencing near the weight pile
(would be nice to sound universal)
not heroin owed
heroin passing messages
heroin left lying around an empire

A colonized intellectual as a guest
in their own hand

It's like a life's work depends
on replicating Birmingham caravans
or particulate Birmingham

One to five shells flying at the state capital
Signed, "Thank you for the resources"

Big band scatting up the throat of a surrogate fascist
in love with their one eyeball
at the parade with tuxedo-colored guns
marrying the cowardice

A re-running white politician
Is born in a Black neighborhood (taken as a stage of history)
Born of a Black Messiah (taken as a foco-biography)
Is born Black (journey'd)
      Legislates in some dimension fused to the side of loud steps

Copper summer riots, but still some blood involved
                        still some necessary slums involved
Ragtag armies masked in western height / in primary emotions
Delight of cocaine both warped and not warped enough / images
   can be cousins
What happens when you step outside the country's sugar gorging?
What good are you all to the world sitting in Heaven?
Who are we going to lay out books for?
Who's going to touch the knives at night and sing to the gaps in
   between shadows . . . gaps between our love?
Who is going to teach our knives to sing *Tobacco Road*
Teach them that they are family

Picture a Black socialist in a perfected boneyard
               in a tributary boneyard
               whispering to cheekbones
               dimming the wind
A Black socialist who will live for one hundred years in this
   graveyard to make this point / that we're in too much pain for
   naming ceremonies . . . that ancestors need to inflict on the
   world our continuity . . .

A thousand good deeds decorate the 20-year police precinct janitor
A janitor (who called it) . . . who knee-slides, but not like you
Telling you of a half-dead humanism to pass the time

A math teacher and their little red book
"I used to dream of revolution . . . and even enjoy the dream"

Factory of Wrists

White people are still in love with whiteness, right? Why, it's no torture nor nightmare to them at all . . .

North american holiday? Because they left your family intact for the weekend?

Continent? No. Continental hate banner? Maybe . . . that's the production that takes over the birds . . . The government senses shape and color again . . . The country has a breathing problem. Cannot concentrate on both capitalism and breathing. Cannot escape its underpass proletariats . . . Cannot deliver us from a traveler's spiritualism.

I'll admit that this is what pain makes me think of . . .

What does it profit to gain the world and lose the sea, man? . . . You can't tell anybody that you're important . . .

Farther . . . just a little farther . . . there . . . do you feel that? Yeah, that's the church traded in for visual art . . . that's some arrogant cotton . . .

The corner and the alley are from the same species, but different symbol within a poem. Historically, more history has come to its transformation in alleys, but corners may be ascending.

Just ask a wharf Elegba, you can gasp for air and still be our leader . . . still be the teacher before the dream

For the Sweetest Laugh I've Ever Known

I close my eyes
    one floor beneath the Five-Spot

Walking a hundred circles in front of a museum photograph

I trusted you
And loved trusting you
And write poems about trusting you still

In Mississippi, I lived a couple non-walkable blocks from a
    juke house
Never did work up enough courage to start the love poem
    there

I'm walking through the Lower East Side with you

                              Perfectly

Trimming a third city
B and C Avenue flowers that work shadow-wise
I asked mother earth for your hand

I'm already in the ground

Kick Drum Only

All street life to a certain extent starts fair

Sometimes with a spiritual memory even
      Predawn soul-clap / your father dying even

Maybe I've pushed the city too far
                  My sensitivities to landfill districting and
          minstrel whistles / modal gangsterism
            white supremacist graffiti on westbound railguards
                    — all overcome and reauthored

revolutionary violence that chose its own protagonists
or muted stage of genius

The garbage is growing voices
Condensed Marxism
For warrior-depressives
Underpasses in their pockets
Because they just might be deities
Or a decent bid on the Panther name

A merciful Marxism

Disquieted home life
Or metaphor for relaxing next to a person
Who is relaxing next to a gun

I stare at my father for a few seconds
Then return to my upbringing

Return to the souls of Ohio Black folks

Revolution is damn near pagan at this point

You know what the clown wants? The respect of the ant.
Wants to interpret pain only
wants your old soul to turn young
see ancestors in broad daylight
wants to pull a .38 out of a begging bowl
wants me to hurt my hand on this pen

I am not tired of these rooms; just tired of the world that gives
    them a relativity

My only change of clothes prosecuted
The government has finally learned how to write poems

shoot-outs that briefly align . . .
that make up a parable

Parables likc, white bodies are paid well
Do white men actually even have leaders?
Are all white people white men?

A rat pictures a river
Can almost taste the racial divide
Can almost roll a family member's head into a city hall legislative
   chamber
Knows who in this good book will fly

> *All I do is practice, Lord*
>> *I have decided not to talk out of anger ever again*

Met my wife at the same time I met new audience members for our
   pain
We passed each other cigarettes and watched cops win
A city gone uniquely linear
Harlem of the West due a true universe

> *"I will always remember you in fancy clothes," my wife said*
>> *so here I sit . . . twisting in silk ideation*

My rifle made of post-bellum tar
My targets made of an honest language
This San Francisco poetry is how God knows that it's me whining
Writing among the lesser-respected wolves
Lesser-observed militarization
Dixie-less prison bookkeeping / I mean the California Gray-coats
   are coming
lynch mob gossip and bourgeois debt collection
I mean, it's tempting to change professions mid-poem

in a Chicago briefing, a white sergeant saying, "blank slate for all
    of us after this Black organizer is dead"
standard academics toasting two-buck wine at the tank parade

bay of nothing, Lord

nuclear cobblestones, gunline athleticism
and the last of the inherited asthma
children given white dolls to play with and fear
facial expressions borrowed from rich people's shoestrings

> *I can hear hate*
> *And teach hate*
> *And call tools by people names*
> *And name people dead to themselves*

no one getting naturalized except federal agents soon
carving the equator into throats soon

I'm sorry to make you relive all of this, Lord

pre-dawn monarchy
friends putting up politician posters then snorting the remainder
    of the paste
minstrel scripts shoveled into the walls by their elders

my children sharpening quarters on the city's edge

> *For these audiences*
> *I project myself into a ghost-like state*

For these gangsters, I do the same

every now and then, we take a nervous look east

Sleep becomes Christ
Sleep starts growing a racial identity

do you ever spiral, Lord?
has the gang-age betrayed us?
be patient with my poems, Lord

So much pain
       there is a point to crime . . .

    There has to be if race traitors come with it
        Lord, is that my revolver in your hand?

Better presidents than these have yawned at cages
Have called us holy slaves
Filled the school libraries with cop documentaries

Baby, I don't have money for food

I have no present moment at all

Soldier Clothes

Millions pretend
        that water is white noise

The people part of memory
           sleeps beside a soda can

                      or two

Beside a chair's-eye view of revolution

Chemical America
        becomes human enough
           to wear a wedding room
                then no form further

Pennies for the Opera

Our perfect confidence in the sun

In commemoration

every tambourine a thousand miles in every direction
                        playing in a California rent party

rattlers dancing and bleeding over God's non-whitened skin

waiting for the cornfield to shrug
                we are forgetful
                but your ancestors nevertheless

slowing down the poem to the speed of sweet light

the speed of bed-less deaths
the bones of fast friends near a pile of first fruits

                                a pile of imperialist failings

oppressor and oppressed give their guns the same nickname

underground working-class sort of goes back to school
                        sort of studies revolution

The summer belongs to itself now
As does a sharecropper's God
As does the death mask

Real advice from Malcolm
Real rose chords over my Memphis skeleton
      a tenor part before dying
      playing to our waning blood pressure
      our penny-plated gun (the last of the space-time) tucked

white people would have sold us standing naked on anything
      sold us off a huge garden crystal
        or peacock feather
          would have sold us off of a stack of doowop
            records if they could
          would have sold us off of the perfection of
            the cosmos

Forestry of drug paraphernalia
      suburb spikes in the grass
      syringe jungle like a sick bed's sick bed

      execution needle that became a society's bottle neck
      preamble noose-talk
      or nuclear scientist thanked for their work

      Activists who don't scream Black power / rather Black
         component

A painful season
Season gone sentient
      and well-dressed
      taken as a whole
      taken in puppet skin

a sentient Sunday that married fifteen sticks of dynamite

we are houseless now
    and dancing our waistlines into a courtroom floor

Atlantic Ocean throwing my voice onto the city weeds
City weeds of the other other confederacy

I would double down on this poem
    on this gang friendship

signs of apocalypse in all directions
    I would run this poem into the ground

on my fifth skipped meal
    "today, Lord, we become even better friends"

Dollar-store notebooks in a mass context
Pen cap full of bullets
California color line as played out with necro protest types who
    sleep on the other other earth
While we are waiting to shoot on a muralist's behalf
    This waiting to shoot: an old man's truancy of sorts
    or tear stain on a Panther pamphlet

houseless bookseller speaking about little Bobby the conqueror

A crisis of open-air corrections
Chemical extradition
And war songs wearing off

Around the corner from South Texas
You pretended that prison is a river
You married your american cop

Black skin / white mantras

Like normal-speed bullets changing a normal life

Like walking back to the united states in defeat

Smooths

She pushes my soul back into my tear ducts
Her classical bravery speaking on behalf of a playful love
Our house is ascending
I held you in every room
        and in every room right now
commenting on the sea line
putting boots to whirlwind
every place she turned my life into decent artwork
"Maybe my second life came too soon"
Poet stops writing secretly
instrument of a new people
a slice of the universe enjoying its exhaustion
Poet offers help to everyone they see
"Maybe my third life came too musically"
She is loved back by her books
Did you come all the way back from
the Harlem Renaissance
just to have a word with me?
I am for sure
        your poetry too

Knees Next to Their Wallets

Fast cash smuggled through my infant torso
                        I arrived smiling

    Coral check-cashing spots seal my eyes

Hearing voices,
        but none of them sing to me

            I am lucky to be a metaphor for no one

                Washing my face with the memory of water
                    my back to the edge of a chessboard
                I mean I'm settling into a petty arrest record
        with my face laid flat on an apartment kitchen table

                    Mississippi linoleum begins

    government plants braiding together breathing tubes

    A Greek philosopher takes the path of least resistance
                The bronze corporation age dawns

                Citizen council rest haven
                Coachable white nationalism
            In boardrooms, they ask if county line skin
                can be churned directly into cornflakes

                A senate's special chain gang mines

our neighborhood for evidence of continent unity

Makes a mess of the word "kin"

Makes a war report
out of a family's secret chord progression

Makes white people geniuses

Lynch-mob freaks rehearse their show tunes
in the courthouse walls that they take for mirrors
Rehearse for a president's pat on the head
a pat on the head
that they take for audience laughter

A lot of "sir"s in the soup
A lot of speed

Treaty ink stained teeth
write themselves a grin

Imperialist speech writers' grins
boil over in my ink-riddled mind

A non-future dripping with real people
I mean, real people . . . Not poem people

A street with no servants somehow
A soul singer/somehow in the west
Consolation eternity

or
The poor man's fish order
This half of a half of a spirit
Or husk of a messiah

Religious memorabilia made from the wood of a
prison farm fence

For sibling domestic colonies and the
not-for-profit Tuesday meltdowns
We do straightforward time

every 28 hours
the house dares the slave

Doesn't matter if you name a building Du Bois a thousand times

System makes a psychic adjustment

What really turns you into a sergeant mention
Turns you into a landslide of sirens

layout sketches passed between deacons

Plot twists provided by white beggars
In a Black city
The fathers who Reagan flicked
Kicking garbage thinking about rates of production
Notebooks dangling out of car windows

We go the way of
Now-extinct hand gestures
Mediterranean sandals and underground moods
in tandem

I mean, whoever I am today is still your friend

Crooked cops and crooked news junkies
Amadou Diallo is your mind on military science
Mario Woods the gang enhancement they even put on God

If you turn down the television low enough, you can hear
San Francisco begging for more war profiteering

We will not live forever, but someone out there wants us to
As mice pouring through an hourglass
In Olympus, Babylon
Or Babylon, Olympus

subway car smoke session
making its way into an interrogation room
(Maybe it is all just one room.
It's definitely all just one smoker)
Live from your
monotheistic toy collection
Poor people writing letters
near books about Malcolm X
Ice pick in the art
new floorboards for
Watts prophecy

Pen twitching over scrap paper
Pen tweaking while
Smoothly a bus driver delivers incarcerated children

The Lord's door opens

the shape of state emblems

Somewhere on the west coast, the third neighbor over doesn't care about Maroon history . . . and you've gone and forced his hand. This whole city started with an arranged strata matrimony. Middleclass-ness, if the sky were to belong in a poem. The seat next to me is a place of panic. Cops excitedly thinking, "Boy, my rock-n-roll is going well." Riding human flesh through the city. Cars bouncing off of your best friends. A chattel-man consciousness bogged down; a death of white purpose mainly. Devil, you gonna show up here and do what? Show me how bad your feelings were hurt . . .

Born to Local Precincts

I like this side of the city

       the side that Queen mothers watch over

tutoring the commune meetings
bringing prosperity to the revolution

holy, holy handshakes / the drums you love while kneeling
                  or unintelligible chariot-talk

      Good suggestions on all sides of my friend's passing

Lower the correct casket this time

Sneak the same eyes into your master's stomach
      Your dangerous imagination running with a factory rat
      sardine-tin rex
      revolution colors on the soles
      from walking with a knife over astronomy books
              in the new South living room

We got married in secret at the Black Power conference
Wearing modest underground clothes
Made in Black San Francisco

          I don't think I'm being followed, momma
              maybe studied a little

maybe I can sketch you, Lord

or at least the veins of red in my eyes

I Make Promises Before I Dream

No unclaimed, cremated mothers this year

Nor collateral white skin

No mothers folding clothes to a corporate park preamble
No sons singing under the bright lights of a lumberyard

Quantum reaganomics and the tap steps of turning on a friend

New York trophy parts among
    the limbs of decent people
        Being an enraged artist is like
            entering a room and not knowing what to get high off of

My formative symbols / My upbringing flying to an agent's ears
                I might as well be an activist

                Called my girlfriend and described
      All the bottles segregationists had thrown at me that day

      Described recent blues sites and soothing prosecutions
                I feared for my poetry

You have to make art every once in a while
    While in the company of sell-outs
    Accountant books in deified bulk
    Or while waiting for a woman under a modern chandelier

Or in your last lobby as a wanderer

The prison foot races the museum

My instrument ends

I mean, what is a calendar to the slave?
Also, what is a crystal prism?

"He bought this bullet,
bought its flight,
then bought two more"

Lower-Class Artist Imagines

Grip my heart tighter, Lord
                    Help me write on this sleeve . . .

                 like listening to Nina Simone later in life

                   The poet takes over for his former self:
               the secret to writing poems is to not deflect.
If you do not know anything fretted about the color blue,
               don't go calling yourself a child at heart.
      If you have never improvised an elevator ride,
               don't go calling yourself in need of prayer.

Grace be to gang tattoos

a reagan meeting adjourns and modern plant life begins
                   along with dry out-of-body insight

                 strange fake forest in
                     a poor person's bird atrium

                     bark around the Mississippi mixtape or
carceral state mythology of a factory's first Black Chaplain

Rotted food staring at a child
The minor progressions of revolution
               drumming Molotov fills
               three quarters and a floor stain staring as well

white children selling a child

(I mean I was there the night that
                San Francisco disappeared)

Think of me when the sun dies

Half man on scratch paper
Half pickpocket with flailing arms
                double fisted
                Alabama in my Paris
                I am an alcoholic in search of history books

                        ruining the light rail in search of
                                history books
                        (I am limping to poetry)

Along with a caste of haves-adjacent
        A slave deck blossoms sweet baby Easter blood

                Maybe loss of crossroad
                along with unprovable music theory
                        (the poem turns into absolute political failure)

You know, not for nothing,
        the way you all like to blame the devil for every fallen
                intellectual
                        every repast fistfight

for every 28 hours in hurricane america

blame him for every ballot burning

for every shallow pot, pan and murder-man
for every government plant, sloppy musician, and federally
        flagged artist

for every floor plan of capitalists' emotive geometry
                and private schools' private anthems
                        for every kid in a cage

the way you all blame him, man, the devil must be in the sky too

                eyes lowered in the land of the blind

                        a mumbler with a gun / I am the worst
                        of your weapons, Lord

                                Won't you put
                                a space heater
                                in my grave

The devil must have really needed to be a person

I'll split it with you . . . my terrible last will and testament

Muscle instructions for surviving the racism of the human family

Stronghold geometry
    (The lesser vehicle)

Against Stateline geometry
    Neo-confederate spectacle like . . .
    New England's most natural years in the slave trade

A guru in a flooded Louisiana prison
A seventh son
    who knows that he will live the rest of his final day alone
Passes mysticism back to God
    "You put a poet here . . . at the end of this bitter wish-list"

Some words before self-immolation

His mind like a backstage for a multitude
Words like a needle in a stack of throats

Hundred-foot heartbeat, baby, these muddy shoes

    "I play with the geniuses . . . really show myself the future"

Diving like a lazy eye into night
    lazy eye reinvented for a molasses ether

Is it too much to ask to forget pain

the music is helping, momma

Only made of light now . . . like an autobiography ends

Laid out on the street with the rest of the 5/8 fodder
He's cab driver to the world
        Some harsh words

"You know the universe so well . . . lost in your mother's
    thoughts . . . then why did you let the coke pusher go?"

No, it's a beautiful tide
        These dogs of imperialism
I'm happy that they found each other in this rubber-sun
    promised land

"You all really let them hire you right in front of God"

lazy eyes giving him an ovation

        an escape art

No One Gets Away with Mythology

I look at my floors
and I want to put a president there

I don't know too many more words
than this group therapy is pulling out of me . . .
                    pulling out of all of this mix-up murder on television

Gray market tantrums of a typical aristocracy's day in the Afrikan sun

                    The big day on the continent . . . now rotting and local

We will be dancing on that corner forever (an abomination to the
    grandmothers)

You start as a toddler hermit
Pay taxes then pique the interest of God

Deal with your convictions on the way to the racism downtown

                    Who do you want to be when the elders come?
                    When we make the north a souvenir?

                    What breakup are you wishing for?
    Which parallel of cannibalism you might make your amateur music
                    from?

Rainmaker's set about death slowly slang'd

Or no . . . I get it . . . you all want the feeling of a poem
A junkie's trumpet in the refrigerator whose description is
    unmanipulated by the ego

    And why not?
    They will put three apartments in the swamp
    and run you out of this nation-state

    Revolutionaries at the bottom of the scrapyard bathtub
            (the impression swamps made on street people)

King stomach, keep america away from your drug habit / walk
    your drug habit to the light

Schoolteachers . . . no more than bourgeois shadows
cast in an empty convert hall

Flipping obituary pages in your face
Here is your hordes-proposal
or
Anglo-closure
Dutch immunity
Elevators diagonal-ing in

Becoming famous among racist psychopaths

Cokeheads in blue

                    "Come here, convict little"

"Come to idolatry," say the dead

A rookie . . . sent me to the imagination of a nurse station
I changed the music at my own repass

You might actually make it to the bandstand
simple magnetism, this God

Intracommunal forgiveness

　　　May a good universe take us all

Pray They Remain Formless

Listening in Minton's Playhouse until my fingers hurt
A blues turnaround that walks over the dead white bodies —
   a rite of return

Modern lynching, my love . . . one confidence too many . . .
   God reading your chapter to the world

              You know what else comes with a high price?
This pool table's southeast pocket / better placement in a gang war
              I've been bested beneath the underdog
       Looking at this pool table (a poor man's skygazing)
                  Flash backs rapid
                  Flash at the future
               Leader versus shooter

             Headdresses on our bones

           Thug religion — can't take you to a pastor
Black life — somewhere between ransom and capture

         Wash dishes in this restaurant with me, baby

        Black proletariat bathed in late evening likenesses
              God kills who God owes

               Hear absolute power
        A few minutes of a chest plate theft

In these cramped psalms

Regathering around our bones

Newly Arranged Appetite

Field of grass on the radiator
               when you played

rhythming razors
hand pulled into an american institutionalization
       dragging a century across a tobacco leaf
          making the mountain of painkillers a secondary definition

                            but money is green?

you are lying in the hospital for a week thinking about the
    various distances of love

also the various distances of
what police are actually doing — Mason-Dixon line standing up
    straight
Brochure of a liquor store on the corner
Identity climate like a karmic stream that goes hexagonal in the sky
Cash crop / You die

                 Seventh street siren inviting you into a paint can
                 Hip hop born already 8 years old in a lotus flower

We just want to know who gave the devil a protection spell

white mask students of the left
sipping hibiscus whisky
European boots masquerading as relationships to trees

heartfelt education of a modern slave

— Scene 3

Kill Kings
Eat Thrones

Consciousness in big Broadway letters
Closing the street to the New York 21

The Atlantic Ocean nearby licking South Carolina like art for the
    shrine. Like the streets are irrelevant.

Spirit world about Black people
by Black people
on the canvas
and the distance between
the hand and the canvas

You fasten six strings to a spitting Cobra

Your .40 is supportive of all art-making. It's an epoch if the streets
    say it is. A junkie stands up for God. It's an instinct of talent. A
    coup on Seventh.

— The true meaning of numbers

To organize millions

Like the ruling class have a child (a ticket taker to the wealth)
        The floor map between coal miner and in-crowd is easy to
           describe

The challenge is to take all of these imperialist hybrids
And pen stomp them into an apartment staircase
                        to yearn for cosmic proof

            to recruit a soldier every day that you are alive

you start sleeping on the floor with your art . . . with the
    vigil-world with a nonchalant horn-personhood
or decent liver for this causality
            stuffing pollution into your pockets
                    balancing jewelry on this poem

Clocked In Still Starving

My money being
The nonviolent part of rage
A kind of courtesy worship
Or caste-system blues

Bullet casings in the comb
I learned their language immediately
I watched an animal explode into hundreds of flags

Judging by my wounds
The government has counted me in

Face to face
With a police officer's family history
My anecdote is only just beginning

Fomenting Poems

I've come to realize that my people are in check, Lord

Warden network television — amateur Romans — an
   instrumental that slows down the senses

The police are always american / anywhere on earth   blistering

The devil's squatters

dehydration takes hold of the police state

I have other depressions

I didn't have too many relationships along the way . . . Society was
   everywhere

                              Defining the mercy after a water riot

Brandishing insomnia, I have my first conversation of the decade.
   Confidant of the earth now.

"Baby, if God doesn't care about what you're writing, it is time to
   un-die."

                              What's on Malcolm's mind these days

                                        Lord, talk to her for me
                              Tell her that my murder is all but assured

And my train will come to me walking
Lord, allow me to smooth the coat over her shoulders
A few more times

Two Sides Fight

Domestic colony
       in increments of eclipse

Shiny incarcerated writer blocked by
Empty San Francisco wallet blocked by
Gangsterism / and other coherent outcomes
Hymnal outcomes /

Picking through a chest cavity,
a vulture continues his muffled monologue within a man's chest
says, "I wonder who fought for you, good sir. Look here, I got a
    flush.
A lot of paint chips and pink slips in this rib cage. City fumes /
    gardened and groomed. We really do pray with our two hands
    on two different floors / Let me meddle just a little bit more."

Increments of childhood
       double consciousness or two metronomes in a bar
              Now one thought jumping to a gray wall to die
                    — One peasant against the world

Childhood peeling from the juvenile hall walls

             "at this point what is anyone doing in america?"

my membership card in a non-Black union blocked by
pieces of tusk on a workshop floor
God not in my hands /

God not in my comedy
        just my shallow breath in an old donut shop's spoon

                my dry-Leninism

        naming my poisons after political theories
                      names like:
                  Gray Man Minstrel
           and Bolivia Back Then

The Cycle of Black Mercy

Well I have at least fallen around love
Reading poems next to my friend with Loisaida fire escapes in
    their teeth
Talking about the gun I'm going to bring to the segregation
Trying to protect children with poems / protect these store runs
Avenue nights as a hospital bard
I can't make out the system of craft
Is this run the house dust circuit / are these abandoned houses of
    various rank
art here like karma-less soldiering

Falsifying my first solo on this stage / on this rickety enemy-ness
Ladies and Gentlemen, here to make some warmongering of your
    night
                                these receipt-paper poems
Adorning my red eyes with a self-inflicted fatherhood
over-policed eyes
state impressionism bouncing back and forth between skin and
    ski mask
an emotional range or wobbly self-portrait
amongst these church giants
calcified personas present / grown man depression
scraping cotton against uptown silhouettes / see in their shadows
    all manner of bombs
king of the poems, baby
genuine marvel of the history of poems
welcome to the mild bourgeoise
revolution street fairs / our weariness

well-proven socialism / the death of both your and my hip-hop,
    Lord
make your greenback ruling-class confetti / art somewhere in this
earn stripes with three hands / cut God off of your shirt
look out at the world from the inside of an ink stroke
I don't mind the Mississippi steel, sir, but may I have a saxophone
    from a different city
bright lights / lethal injection routine / last words / Is My Family
    Here
take all disrespect as the universe in motion
I write poems today
I kill america today

       Five-year anniversary of my style
       (swamps talking / midsize activist files like songs sitting
         under the street /
       Slave castles growing and growing /
         keeping notebooks alive the wrong way /
           human temper sitting still)

Going to Afrika in mysterious ways
the harp that turned the hand toward the Founding of Chicago

You know what my trick is, grandson?
I am weak first
Before anything, I first become weak

Kick a hatchet down the street / then all around a city
a grandmother's Milwaukee
or the gods my grandmother robbed

fresh faces in the spirit house / a spirit house we've put behind
the sun

We have God's permission to make a plan

Gradually, the poem becomes decently empty

You know, be weak
Let the ability to write slip
until only one fingertip is left on the handle
then, in a flash, return with a slave castle in a cup of change

"Ladies and gentlemen:
We assure you that tonight's entertainment is not judging you . . .
We paid them . . . really well"

And Other Themes

Started the record over
An agreement of old souls
Your hands chasing the bass line through air — and it's easy going
For you, three street lamps at the window
With gifts — the rest of our lives
The dresser bends (being just another form of light)
I missed your call
Lost in the memory of your waste — my mind might
Actually become free
Out of body her room moves me
Do you mind if I live for you tonight?

No Stars Over the Trenches Tonight

Overplaying R&B war records, a surrealist lies to their self
Staring into someone's reactionary soul all day
Staring at a citizenship meant for lying
    "Well my, my. You are a city"
        crumbling down around geniuses
           who have a better manner with world war bricks
preparatory city interested in that fact / pan-ruling-class staging
released from their godhood / audience levitating with drone
   strikes

               Addictions crawl comfortably
          (never using their own arms / just
     class membership / cogs become europeanized bullies)
          your problems relentlessly mine
       same reason they say Sioux City will keep you

Flock music moving in from a fossil distance
Even the importation of other planets

      I'm a little slow with the pen tonight
      Some object will have to be animated now
      Or stilt-walkers who come to kill me
      My door and its frame laid exit-side down on the street

Skeletal betrayal . . . even my insanity

One abyss wearing off and another abyss opening its arms

these white civilians are deeply connected to slavery
and they write better than me

"It's like doing time in a drum-less society"
Modern people mutilating each other uptown
        — Please put all of your flags on this uptown sidewalk
And allow anyone their revenge —
        Some revenge even featuring a fight down to the prophet
            rearing
        "I hear they got a better God in Mississippi"

I am begging a wino for help sorting out my problems like they
    are the only ancestor left in my pocket

        An object now animated in two poles
america in handwriting like breakfast littered

        "They don't know how cosmic it is down here where we
    take every imperialist decade personally. Man, this sewer is a
    poem."

Our father the tenement vendetta

Has the poem started yet?
I will tuck your shirt into the earth

I am / I am not one of you

> Flowers follow us all around a hospital
> (silhouettes shackled to God)

The carpenter's wood saw is crawling through the walls, right?

> Calling your cold sweats the night that heaven stood still.
> Wail at the wall until all your questions are answered
> by good people. Profess an estimated love.

> A friend fighting for their life

> Elders laughing us out the lobby

The Chicago Prairie Fire

First, I must apologize to the souls of the house
       I am wearing the cheekbones of the mask only
              Like a pill bottle whose name is yours
              Name tagged on the side of a factory of wrists

Teeth of the mask now

Back of the head of the mask now

    New phase of anti-anthropomorphism fending for real faces

Stuck with one of those cultures that believes I chose this family

                    I am not creative
           Just the silliest of the revolutionaries

          My blood drying on
          my only jacket

          The police state's psychic middlemen
     evangelizing for the creation of an un-masses
                an un-Medgar
           blood of a lamb less racialized
           or awesome prison sentence
                Good God

          A right angle made between a point
             on a Louisiana plantation

and a 5-year-old's rubber ball
3 feet high and falling
like a deportee plane
to complete my interpretation
(of garden variety genocide)

I am small talk
about loving your enemies
a little more realistically

About paper tigers
And also gold . . .

I need my left hand back
I broke my neck on the piano keys
Found paradise in a fistfight

Maybe I should check into the Cuba line

Watching the universe's last metronomes
some call Black Jacobins

Just wait . . .
These religions will start resigning in a decade or two

Some colorfully
Some transactionally

In a cotton gothic society

Class betrayal gone glassless / I mean ironically / my window
started fogging over too
Wondering which Haiti will get me through this winter
Which poem houses souls

Which socialist breakthroughs
Breakthroughs like ten steps back
Then finally trying stillness

Like introducing Gabriel Prosser to Thelonious Monk

I remember childhood
Remember the word "Childhood" being a beginning

Scribbling on an amazing grace

I rented this body from some circumference of slavery

Remember being kicked out of the Midwest

Strange fruit theater
Lithium and circuses
Like-minded stomachs
The ruling class blessing their blank checks with levy foam . . .
with opioid tea
Sentient dollar bills yelling to each other pocket to pocket
Cello stands in the precinct for accompanying
counterrevolutionaries

My mother raised me with a simple pain

A poet loses his mind, you know, like the room has weather
Or first-girlfriend gravity

"The difference between me and you
Is that the madness
Wants me forever"

A pair of apartments
        Defining both my family
        And political composure

Books behind my back
Bail money paved into the streets

Playing:
Euphoria
Euphoria
Cliché

                        Bracing for the medicine's recoil

            Sharing a dirty deli sandwich with my friends
                        Black Jacobins
                        Underground topography
                        Of a grandmother's hands

                        Psychology of the mask now

                        Teeth of the mask again

News of the Morning

Shantytown Martin
Accepting soldiers' food and making speeches for the trash fires
Some are worried about Martin
But we are relaxed about him
We keep King close
We bargain the cosmos for our militant lives with him
Keep him with us in Bolivia
The state is going to experience us differently
          No, you can name an army after Martin

Modern Art

I am going to go with the mountain range
I am going to rival marines

Admittedly, I would be no 8th wonder to catch. Walking slowly.
    Lost in a Max Roach speech.
Talking to a Max Roach twin. "So they actually send you to an
    electric chair?"

Monologues written in my heart by a planetary anger not mine
Monologues also written about my heart by the apartheid sick

Apartheid sunrise
Politely asking God to calm down with that big paschal candle
    up there.
Can you call off your talent, Lord?
Your brilliant past
        and brilliant future

Advise me with the golden ratio again

                Get me off the streets

I tried writing my plans slower and with less tension in my
    aging hands
But one low tide snake does not make a mythology tick

Clichés playing me like
a shotgun beat

into the shape of
a saxophone (who am I
besides secondary?)

smokestack jade stone
or a ton of communist optimism

The first time I was arrested, I was twelve years old. I held up the
    european cannonball they handed me for the mugshot. The
    title of this poem is "No one got away." I will end it with a line
    about little arrest records and the luck of an auction chair.

God is in it
        (breaking the 5th wall)

Masses pushing you over the edge into a different kind of masses
                            into a black water joke scheme

civilians inherently federal now

                    You are really not going to offer these people of color
                                    their jaguar masks back?

Middle-age criminals behind a music box / ears flush against
    some fifties' tin
fanatic tempos of Lutheran evictions and prison reform / fodder
fanatic tempos
like people nailing their hands to wood thinking they are nailing
    yours
let's all sing along to the steel driving

like pigeons over a jackhammer
out pops a north american adoptee
avoiding revolutionaries for a living

Then some road is pathed (bitter storyboards in the brick pile)

Then some liberal bigotry and McCarthy hearings in the hospice

　　　　　　"a lot less infinity these days for coloreds"

Everybody is a gangster rapper until a real-life Mack truck plows
　　through a Venn diagram
(to make a point, there's only two ways that sea salt could have
　　gotten on your skin)

　　　　　　"Hush your strange poems now"

I am a schoolteacher looking up
at a falling american bomb
　　　　　　　　— The cause turns 50 years old

I wonder how Black utopias would look if they existed
On the same plane that I tend to fall in love on

Away from the cold, hard cash
Away from the fanatic tempo of mispronounced tender and
　　secret junkie ideology
Like there are rose petals attached to that ballot
(In love with an elected official

who checked on your grandmother for two days) . . . Roses in
the rap water

What is a dreamscape to Denmark Vesey?

Denmark
To be his people's first love

You can't fool Denmark
With your apartheid nativity scene
like cups of water in a pentagon conference room
I can hear supervisors clapping from here

america builds time a fascism

Closer than a description of skin, I am finally ready, sir, for a
worse cage

Growing up, I thought talking was only what God did. But you
have to be careful with those type of conclusions. Twelve years
old. Noticing that there were no windows for this white
kindness. Wondering if without aggression do birthdays exist.
I will be the last important fact of revolution. The long walk
from magnolia tree to child who won't say a lonesome word.

Third in the World

Societies wander together like hopeful drops of a virus

Citizen-testaments bent on offing me

     A nation of breadwinners to hold me back

like it's a Brink's, I wrinkle the concrete sometimes
like flesh, my Martin Luther King permanence
               turning away from a podium into the reeds
like God is the dangerous twin

Black August to the mountain top
     balcony on my bedroom floor

They steal you from the earth itself and suspend you and your
    broken neck
from their fullest euphoria
            from the loyalty oath of their gray superstitions
                  loyalty oath of their agrarian reform

I return to my mother
     completely disrespected

For peeling the heat off of purgatory, they kill poets like me
    Walk me away from my poems; never to be heard from again

in this final industrial complex or
bloodlines picked over / picked through

A sport in spiritual death or your devil at least half made

Police become a pretty word

I'm reading a lynch mob's shoestrings like they were tea leaves
Teaching you how to write about cities

It's the 25th century in the mirror, people
Tyranny against your chump change
You're a chump to be mocked even with a gun in your car

A cubit of needlework spelled tomb for the proletariat
The relapse ministry

Talented people curled up in the fetal position next to a
    diamond dying

Just another service day in the theatrics of tea house fascism
In a bouquet of surveillance cameras

In the poverty of God

New blue eyes
Corpses of water
Newly potted presidency or one big shiny coin
if you ask an animated capitalism and other non-literal voids

Killing is white freedom
The deification of hyphens
Medicine bread and picture shows

Gray protesters in LA
Guests of our ink
drop-kicking roses in a graveyard
D.C. mink

Like a stone torn in half
     the pen advances despite cia guideposts
     despite non-Afrikan pasts and futures

A metaphorical but not surreal day in a horn-ridden life
horn player improvising King

               Like a radio prize fight featuring Shango himself
                  A real hand sweeps the land of racism

                    May I return to the ground
                May I make progress with the gun
                      My Mother Emanuel

They put on music that evening
A swinging type body language
For you to drink with fermented five-dollar bills

For your body language, some applause
My past stomach lining

     Neither a good thing nor a bad thing
     Like being psychic on the way to a lethal injection

It will sit you down with Lady Day
Lady Day leading youth who surrendered their souls to Afrika
    too soon

Polity thought floating in the cup of water she saved me
Accessing my stomach
Accessing the love of the american lynched

Coat sleeves wooden and avalanching to the wrist
Our Mother Emanuel
avalanching to the sharp keys

Pain . . . the deal you make with pain

        a piano makes sense for them
        laying hands on the world gradually.
        addressing the bend of necks on the streets of the North.
        travelers sailing in pain / repeating pain in the North.

ten trigger fingers on that piano
if Harmony would have me

Putting a hundred fights on every direction offered her
                Lady Day leaning on trees again
                        recruiting the countryside itself

Lay your plan out on this lightning
Make your poems the corner pocket of men

I've greeted the Blues itself

america may clean my dead body, but will never include me

there goes the poet — killing without killing — don't mind this
   . . . this painting of your language

may I be a meaningful lynching

a crow's passing

   good and dead by the afternoon

Tongo Eisen-Martin is the Poet Laureate of San Francisco, California. He is the author of *Heaven Is All Goodbyes* (City Lights Books, 2017), which was shortlisted for the Griffin International Poetry Prize and received the California Book Award for Poetry, an American Book Award, and a PEN Oakland Book Award. He is also the author of *someone's dead already* (Bootstrap Press, 2015).